SHORT PUMP
BUMP!

A Lyrical, Spherical, Rhyming Romp Through Richmond

Poems and photos by Angie Miles
Illustrations by Scott DuBar

BELLE ISLE BOOKS
www.belleislebooks.com

ISBN: 978-1-9399306-3-7
Library of Congress Control Number: 2017949626
Printed in the United States

Published by

BELLE ISLE BOOKS
www.belleislebooks.com

in cooperation with 3 Pages Press

Author's Dedication

Photo Credits: Penumbra

This work is dedicated to the many teachers who recognized, respected, and required something of the reader and writer in me: Ann Davis for poetry contests, *Highlights*, Carolyn Haywood, Donald Sobol, and Dewey Decimal; Bess Maxey for discarded book treasures and expressive Lions and Tigers for a very shy girl; Linda Curry for poetry paper and my own writer's corner—despite this seeming more "fanciful" than "true to life;" Octavia Lewis for those *Twenty Froggies* and all the sacred recitations; Peggy Strickland Lankenau for praise and public performances of my poems, plays and songs and for valuing every, single line; Barbara Sturgill for writing prompts, goal-setting, and awakened imagination; Randi Wolf Lauterbach for James Thurber and her Herculean love expressed through unflinchingly high expectations; Barbara Musgrove for girlhood stories, the joy of reading aloud, and the humor of *Cheaper by the Dozen*; Helen Grier for Shakespeare, Anne Frank, and grammar, grammar, grammar; Dave Noechel for intense discussions and for being the perfect thinking, reading, and writing coach, and for e. e. cummings; Karen Norsworthy for a rich cascade of classic American literature and an understanding that the thing imagined is always greater than the thing perceived; and Graham Lester for mischievous yet unassuming humor and for revealing the living luster on the oldest of tales. I say thank you to Toby Friedman for purity of heart that embraces all children and stays true to the child within. Thank you Ed Alexander for *The Case of the Missing Parts of Speech* and for the perfect knowledge that there is music in everyone and in everything. And eternal gratitude to Drina Kay and Lu Armbrecht for confidence in the creative quickening. All that you did stays with me.

Illustrator's Dedication

To my wife, Vidya, who took so much delight in every illustration I did for this book. With special thanks to Angie Miles for reaching out to me and helping me make my dream of illustrating children's books come true.

TABLE of CONTENTS

Opportunity Time

I rise with the sun
On this brand new day.
Opportunity time,
I'm on my way.

I've songs to sing,
And games to play.
Opportunity time,
I'm on my way.

I've stories to write
And rhymes to say,
Masterpieces to paint
In my new beret.

To school, to the park,
The museum, ballet!
Time to make special things,
Time to give some away.

I can share. I can love.
And you know, I just may.
Opportunity time,
I'm on my way.

I'll invent a new something
To shouts of "Hurray!"
I can do anything
With this gift called "today."

It's opportunity time,
And I'm on my way!

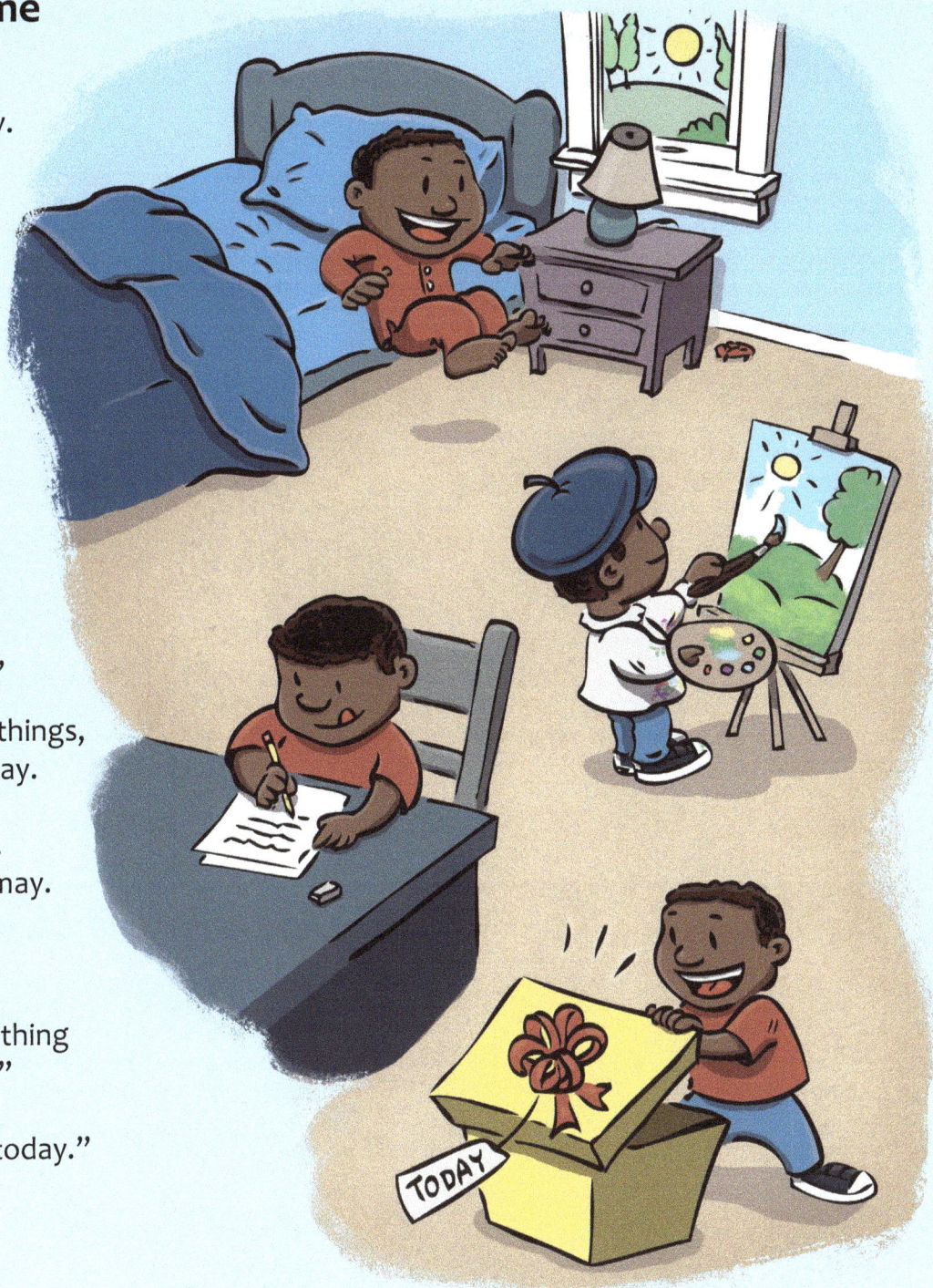

Kidkadoo

It's a kidkaday
At Kidkadoo.
Let's kidkaplay!
Kidkatrain, kidkazoo.

Kidkagirls
And kidkaboys
Find smiling curls
And learning toys.

Read kidkabooks,
Stack kidkablocks.
Kidkascience cooks!
Kidkapainting rocks!

What laughing, happy
Kidkanoise
Among those magic
Kidkatoys.

It's kidkasweet
At Kidkadoo
When I kidkameet
With kidkayou!

To Yen. On behalf of countless kids and families, thank you for the memories. And to all the Kidkadoo staff over so many years, thank you for adding such sweetness to so many childhoods. It was sublime.

Dear Deer

Deer in the driveway,
Deer in the street.
Deer in the places
We don't usually meet.

Deer in the garden,
Deer on the greens,
Next to fake reindeer
And nativity scenes

Deer stopped and staring,
Deer with no fear.
It seems that their numbers
Get bigger each year.

Watch out all drivers!
Unafraid as they feel,
I can almost imagine
A deer at the wheel.

Royal Ribbit

A prince lived on Huguenot Road,
But a spell turned him into a toad.
He asked a young miss
For a magical kiss,
And then Maymont
became their abode.

For the Love of Trains

Trains go chug. Trains go choo.
When the trains go by—
What do I do?

I stop. I listen. I love that sound.
That soul-stirring rumble rolling
smoothly over ground.

Trains chug black,
Red, gray and blue.
When the trains chug by—
What do I do?

Stop. And look. On a trestle so high,
There's a mountain of motion
across a blue sky.

Trains float over water.
Trains fly through the field,
Gliding quickly on the tracks,
They're not winged, and not quite
wheeled.

Stop. Listen!
Hear them roar to where they're bound.
Feel the power of those trains,
Moving mountains over ground.

ASHLAND

Surround Sound

Bubble gum on a train.
Chew. Chew. Chew.
Ask an owl a knock-knock joke...
Who? Who? Who?

ant ant ant ant ant ant ant ant ant ant ant hill

Church Hill Jill

A park near the top of Church Hill
Was loved by a girl named Jill.
One day Jill's friend Jack
Bumped his head with a whack!
But the pretty view cured all his ill.

East End

Richmond Hill. Woodville.
East End. East End.
Tobacco Row. Mr. Poe.
East End. East End.
Do you know Chimborazo?
East End. East End.

A coffee, brunch, or café lunch?
St. John's will teach
That famous speech
Where Patrick Henry
did decree
"I'll have my life with liberty!"
(His words went down in history
For being Revolution'ry!)

It happened in the
East End. East End.
You'll find out if you
just stop by.
East End. East End.
It's all that and a
slice of pie!
East End. East End.

The Ghost of Annabel Lee

Do you remember
Annabel the fair?
And do you care
That she is not there?
No she is not there,
Annabel the fair,
Not there upon the James River.

Oh, the thought of her
And each sailing trip
On our little ship
At a slow, steady clip.
Such a slow, steady clip,
On each sailing trip
Across the lovely James River.

Yes, Annabel Lee,
I long to see.
But where can she be?
Oh, where, where is she?
Gone north, to D.C.
Annabel, hear our plea.
You've left memories upon our James River.
Memories moving upon our James River.

Your true home is on our James River.

Precious Child

Gilpin's child is fair of face.
Creighton's child is full of grace.
Fulton's child knows how to grow.
Fairfield's child is wise, you know.
Hilliard's child is loving and giving.
Flagler's child makes life worth living.
Born winter, summer, spring, or fall,
Each precious child is a gift to all.

This is a love poem for all children. Every child is a treasure and needs to know it. It's also worth knowing that in the best of times and in the worst, good books can be good friends that help us reach a HAPPY place.

Hello Up There

Hello up there!
There's a bird in your hair.
Now why would you wear
A bird in your hair?

Birds belong in the air.
But I don't think you care.
It's awfully rare,
A bird in the hair.

I just wouldn't dare
Have a bird in my hair.
You make a very odd pair
I'm sure people will stare!

I think you should share.
It's only fair.
I would share if I had
A bird to spare.

I want savoir faire,
That certain flair.
But first I'll have to reach up there.
I'll just go get a chair.

11

Easter Bonnets on Parade

Walkers, runners, dancers
Strutting on the avenue.
Some of the things you see here
Seem a little strange.
It's true.

That lady over there
Has her lunch up on her head.
I see fruit and nuts and vegetables.
What's missing?
Just some bread.

And here's a floating hat.
No eyes, no ears, no curl.
A kid is somewhere under there,
But the bonnet is wearing . . .
The girl.

The Flower Lady's here to spread
Some rainbows while it's sunny!
A dog has long, white, fluffy ears.
But that dog is NOT
A bunny.

I hear drums, yet I don't see them.
Just peaceful men and focused boys
Adding heartbeat using buckets,
Filling air with
Joyful noise.

A funny, flapping chick
Goes clucking by on people legs.
And girls in beads and braids
Look like, you know,
Easter eggs!

It's walkers, runners, dancers
Strutting on the avenue.
Easter bonnets on parade,
A springtime party,
Just for you!

The Flower Lady, Jonathan the Juggler, Happy the Artist, Ty-Rone the Kids' Comedian, and Ram Bhagat's Drums No Guns musicians are just a few of the special people who have labored with love to make Virginia a happier and more beautiful place to live.

Jump Rope Chants

1

Butterscotch, chocolate, caramel
I'm sweet like candy.
Can't you tell?
Salsa, cayenne, wasabi
I jump so fast.
You just watch me!
Lightning feet . . .
Jump so sweet . . .
Count on it.
I'm H-O-T!
1, 2, 3, 4, 5, 6 . . .

2

J-U-M-
P!
J-U-M-
P!
Watch a little while.
See my jumping style.
J-U-M-
P!
J-U-M-
P!
I jump from one
To infinity!
1, 2, 3, 4, 5, 6 . . .

3

I wanna wanna jump.
I wanna wanna play.
I'm gonna gonna jump
All day, all day, all day.

4

Uno, dos, tres,
Quatro y cinco . . .
Five times fast,
I go. I go. I go!
Seis, siete, ocho,
Nueve y diez.
Ten times fast,
I'm the best!
I'm the best!

5
One, two heart
With one, two speed.
I'm double-dutch true . . .
One shoe, two shoe.

One, two turn
That's what I need.
I'm double-dutch true . . .
One shoe, two shoe.

Left foot follow the
Right foot lead.
I'm double-dutch true . . .
One shoe, two shoe.

One, two ready
One, two succeed!
Double-dutch,
Double-dutch,
That's what I need!

6
In France they say "sauter," "sauter" . . .
I can jump like the French.
Sauter. Sauter!
To Provence! To Calais!
I can jump to Marseille.
I can jump all day . . .
Sauter! Sauter!
To Bordeaux!
To Lyon! To Normandy!
To the top of Eiffel Tower!
How far can I see!
From Paris back to home!
Jumping rope is child's play!
I can jump like the French.
Sauter. Sauter!

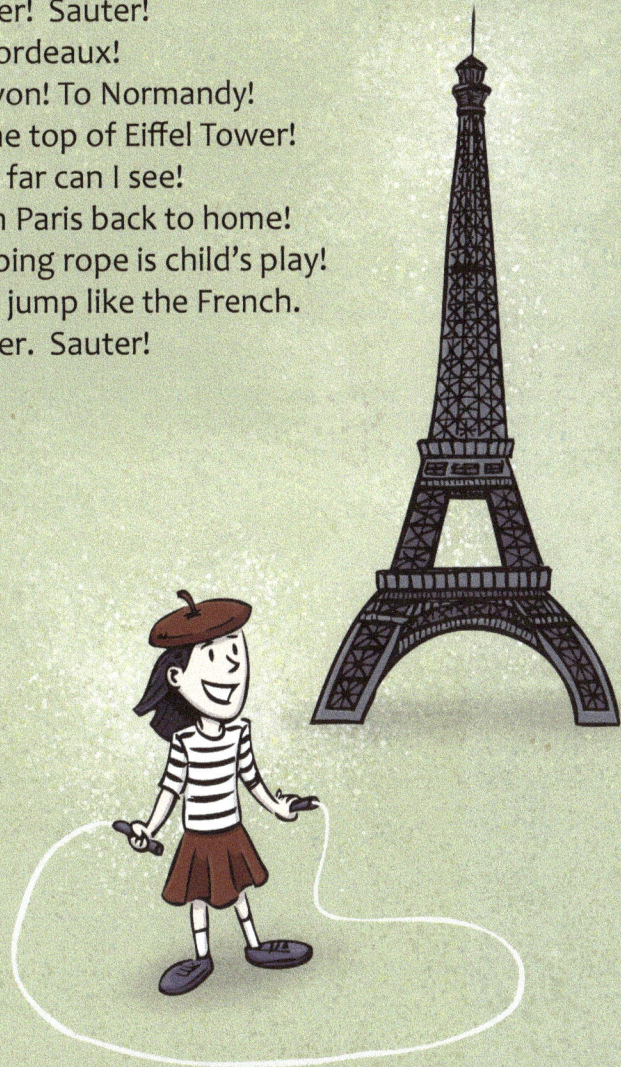

Larry the Lion

Larry is a lion.
He's a lion every day.
He does the thing that's right
No matter what his critics say.

Larry is a lion,
A leader of the pack.
He doesn't make his choices
For a pat on the back.

Larry's a true lion.
He leads by showing what is right.
And by putting others first,
Even if that means a fight.

Brave Larry Lion knows
That it's by service, kings are made.
And that the good we do for others
Is what will never, ever fade.

For Ralph and all such lions, who choose to care beyond what others consider reasonable. It is this integrity and sense of service that help to make greater Richmond part of a greater world, day by day.

Use Your Noodle

There once was a Chesterfield youth
Who thought he was losing a tooth.
He stuck in a noodle
And out popped a poodle.
Now do you think this is the truth?

Out to Pony Pasture

Grandpa says
When you're old and tired,
It may be time to go out to pasture.

Well, it's time.

'Cause I'm tired of playing in my room.
And I'm old—almost six-and-a-half!
So I'll just get the picnic basket,
And we can all go out right now.

17

Horse Sense

Whether I want to,
Or whether I'd not.
We stroll from the stable,
Work up to a trot.

Whether I don't,
Whether I try,
We speed right past gallop.
We're starting to fly!

Whether I shouldn't,
Whether I could,
Wait! doesn't slow us.
Whoa! does no good.

Whether reins in,
Whether reins free,
Who's setting the pace?
Why, it sure isn't me!

Whether we win,
Whether we race,
Wildly we run,
Wind whipping my face.

Whether I shout,
Whether I call,
Whinnying loudly,
We head to the stall.

Whether we stop,
Whether we turn,
What is the lesson?
What is it I've learned?

Whether through weeds,
Whether over the fence.
We've winged our way back
Wended by horse sense.

Belle Isle

Belle Isle
makes me smile.
I smile. I smile.
I smile, smile, smile.

I love the fresh air
And with music to share,
The breeze in my hair,
And my comfy chair.
I can't help but smile
All the while.

Where, oh, where?
I'm smiling right there!
Right there
I declare!
On Belle Isle.

It's Belle Isle.
Just my style.
I'm staying a while
To smile
On Belle Isle.

Northern Flights

A jolly elf passed through Park Ginter.
Riding high in his sleigh, got a splinter.
A doc from Ashland
Took it out of his hand,
Said, "Remember to stop by next winter."
("And don't fly so far south of Center.")

Short Pump Bump

There was a young man from Short Pump
Who learned an old dance called the bump.
He danced it so hard
He bumped out of his yard,
And Goochlanded right on his rump.

WELCOME TO
GOOCHLAND
COUNTY

GPS

Bumper to bumper, we're heading west.
The crowds clump home
Each day at sunset.
Go, go, go! We all get gone
As fast as we can get.

A yellow bug car whips out in front.
Hey, guy, no fair!
Our turn!
Red truck zips. Green zooms, black booms!
Cars bunch, crunch, scrunch, and churn.

A two-door, top-down edges by,
And mom sighs, "Wow! Just look at that sky!"
Inching by drive-thrus serving fries with chicken . . .
We're moving closer to our kitchen.
Beyond the movies and the mall,
We might be last, the last of all!

But we won't be the pushy guy,
'Cause we have bigger fish to fry.
Stuck in that stop-go, brake-screech burn,
I think there's something we can learn.
Some choose to whiz and whine and wheeze,
But we stay easy as the breeze.
When there's ranting and racing and rushing to dinner,
The one who gets home SMILING . . .
. . . is the winner.

We Made a Parade

Ameera's the girl
With the long, shiny braid.
We're best friends now,
So we made a parade!

Hayden's got brownies.
He said he would trade.
I gave him my cookies.
We made a parade!

Sgt. Santa was magic
With fresh lemonade.
It tasted so great
That we made a parade!

It's a zillion degrees,
Even here in the shade.
So we put on swimsuits,
And we made a parade!

We head back to school.
Time to start a new grade.
Time to see my old friends.
Time we made a parade!

Not a leaf on the trees,
Not a single green blade,
But there's sun in our hearts
So let's make a parade.
Yes there's sun in our hearts,
So let's make a parade!

WHO... WHAT... WHEN... WHERE... OF SHORT PUMP BUMP!

Opportunity Time

This is a well-known phrase uttered by former Virginia Governor Linwood Holton, who saw every day as an opportunity. In his memoir, *Opportunity Time* (University of Virginia Press, 2008), he spoke of rousing his children each morning with this invitation to take on the day in a big way. By making the most of his opportunities, Mr. Holton distinguished himself as one of the Commonwealth's most accomplished and beloved chief executives.

The Science Museum of Virginia (smv.org) is housed in the former Broad Street Station near Richmond's Fan District. It was commissioned and dedicated under the watch of Governor Mills Godwin, and provides a place where young and old can both explore and develop a sense of wonder about our world.

Kidkadoo

With much love for Yen Huynh, we remember Kidkadoo. Yen opened her store at Virginia Center Commons in 1995 and later became one of the first tenants at Short Pump Mall in 2003. She specialized in toys

that brought joy, fostered learning, and sparked the imagination. We wish Yen the same happiness that she brought to so many as she embarks on her journey in mechanical engineering.

Dear Deer

We say thank you to the Virginia Forestry Department and the Virginia Department of Game and Inland Fisheries who help us keep a healthy balance

among the plants, animals, and people who share our state. And thank you, as well, to the sponsors of Richmond's Grand Illumination for lighting our lives during the dark of each winter.

Royal Ribbit

Much gratitude to Maymont for providing such natural beauty to Greater Richmond and for their enthusiasm about our poetry project. Thank you, too, for the art and the animals, and for keeping us straight on the differences between frogs and toads. We'll see you in the gardens!

Church Hill Jill

We're giving a group hug here to the countless people and professional endeavors that make the view from Church Hill spectacular and our horizons bright. Thank you to all who helped establish Jefferson Park and to all who continue to maintain this wonderful place, from which we can see the expansive beauty of our city.

For the Love of Trains and Northern Flights

There's so much to love about the rumbling, rolling, romanticism of trains. To big, beautiful Amtrak, with all its fascinating history and devoted personnel... and to the beloved Ashland Train Station in the center of the universe, we offer our appreciation.

East End

And here we go with another group hug! Thank you to all who protect, preserve, and promote the history of St. John's Church. It is a national treasure. Also, it's the leaders (Patrick Henry was one of the first) and the artists (Edgar Allan Poe is one of many) who put the "Rich" in Richmond. We acknowledge the sweat, strife, and sweetness of all who made the East End a vibrant place to live and work, and we remember our opportunity time as we contemplate this starry part of our city, shining brightly to the east.

Ghost of Annabel Lee

With another nod to Mr. Poe, one of our most famous residents, we pen this ode to that smooth-sailing ship that once graced Richmond's waters. The Annabel Lee delighted field-trippers, party-seekers, and sightseers, and even hosted weddings. It pulled anchor and headed north in 2004 for a short stint on the Potomac before being sold and recommissioned. Her absence is still lamented by those who spent time on board.

Precious Child

To our educators throughout the region, and to those who give shelter and hope to families in need or in crisis, we salute you. Thank you for never losing sight of the inherent value and limitless potential in every single person. And thank you to Cheryl Burke for overseeing the creation of such a lovely garden … of flowers and of children.

Hello Up There
Out to Pony Pasture
Belle Isle
Short Pump Bump

and Author Bio Image

Thank you to those who have lived greatly, who have sacrificed, shared, and inspired us to remember them in our public places of honor. At a time of heightened discussion regarding the placement of monuments, may we navigate with wisdom, with respect, and with loving consideration for one another. And like children, may we stay open to a little humor and a lot of creative problem-solving in all we do. Thank you, also, to administrators in state and city offices, to the managers in surrounding counties, and to all the varied staff for maintaining the fixtures, facilities, and great escapes in the place we call home.

Easter Bonnets on Parade

Venture Richmond, Inc., Venture Richmond Events, LLC, and varied sponsors of Easter on Parade, you are awesome for bringing us this event each year. May you "keep things hopping with bonnets topping" for years and years to come!

We Made a Parade

There was only one Sgt. Santa, and he belonged to Richmond. For all the gifts and visits to children, for all the families who got a helping hand during tough times, for the stories and the smiles ... and from the many neighbors helped along life's way by Sgt. Santa and "Elf Ruby," we say thank you. Like the sun during a solar eclipse, you may be out of sight, but you still shine. The work you did speaks for you and echoes warmly in our hearts.

GPS

Thank you to attentive and courteous drivers. You make the world a nicer place.

FOR MORE INFORMATION ABOUT
Short Pump Bump! A Lyrical, Spherical, Rhyming Romp Through Richmond
visit www.shortpumpbump.com

While you're there, look for news about public appearances and book signings, and sign up to receive book-related information by email or text!

Also, pick up a copy of the *Short Pump Bump* companion manual, *Short Pump BUMP UP YOUR BRAIN! A Companion Guide for Educators and Parents*, where you will find suggestions for family and educational activities. For more information on literacy support services, visit Angie Miles' HAPPY Reading website, www.happyreading.org.

And look for the *Bump* sequel, *Spring Zing! Another Rhyming Romp Through Richmond*.

About the Author

Angie Miles is a lifelong Virginian who fell in love with the beauty, novelty, and power of words as a young child. She grew up in rural Powhatan as one of ten children, and at the tender age of two was "reading" her first poem, Clement Moore's "'Twas the Night Before Christmas," which she had memorized in its entirety. Her fascination with written and spoken language was enhanced by siblings, who studied and spoke Latin and French, and by beloved elders, who shared lively stories and family histories in their uniquely sumptuous, southern style.

Her professional pursuits have included broadcast journalism, educational consulting, literacy instruction, and a wide assortment of writing projects. She enjoys family life with her friend Brad, who is also her husband, and their four outstanding sons. High on her favorites list are movie marathons, barefoot running, home-cooked meals, happy travel adventures, and quantum physics. She enjoys books, books, books; music; spending time with interesting, caring, ridiculously optimistic people... and whenever possible, helping others fully discover and embrace their highest potential. She hopes *Short Pump Bump!* will remind young and old alike that when we remember to play, we're well on the way to the places we most want to reach, no matter where those places may be.

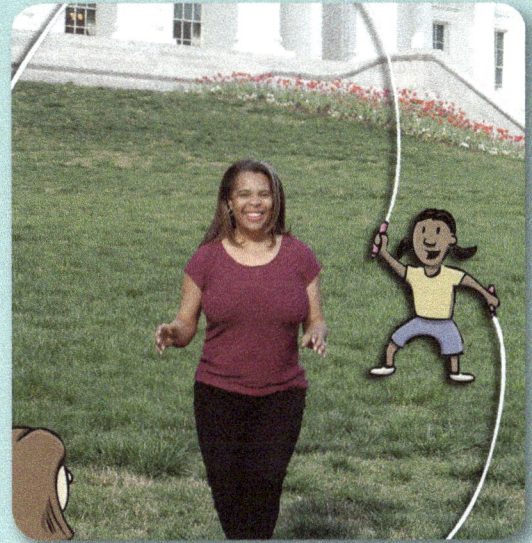

Photo Credits: Myoshi

About the Illustrator

Scott DuBar first started drawing as a small child and never stopped. For eight years, he worked as an illustrator and graphic designer on various charitable projects while living and traveling in India. After returning home, he earned a degree in illustration from Virginia Commonwealth University in 2008. In 2010, Scott began illustrating the poems of Angie Miles for her website, www.happyreading.org. Scott's humorous illustrations appear regularly in several magazines across the country. He currently works out of his home in Charlottesville, Virginia, where he lives with his beautiful wife, Vidya.

www.ingramcontent.com/pod-product-compliance
Lightning Source LLC
Chambersburg PA
CBHW040853100426

42813CB00015B/2789

9 781939 930637